The Power

Of

Influence

Revealed

Jerolin Jackson and Bryant Lloyd

The Power of Influence Revealed

Copyright © 2017, Jerolin Jackson

Book cover design and layout
© MD. Faizan Hasan Qureshi
13-978-0-9989324-1-5

Printed in the United States of America

ALL RIGHTS RESERVED

This book is dedicated to my wife, children and grandchildren whom I love dearly.

Wife:

Leilani Jackson

Children:

Da'Shawn Williams

Sha'Tavia Sanders

Keyon Williams

Serenity Jackson

Grandchildren:

Ke'Yana Williams

Bryce Lloyd

Kaiden Lloyd

Amina Williams

Proverbs 22:6

Train up a child in the way he should go, even when he is old he will not depart from it.

Outline of Contents

Follow me on Social Media @

Www.facebook.com/jerolinj

@Livemylife2Dmax

Jerolin Jackson

livemylife2dmax

Www.themoneymakinggroup.com

Www.jerolinjackson.info

Www.trytvforfree.com

Www.jerolinjackson.com

Www.bit.ly/mycoffeelover

4triadmarketing@gmail.com

jacksonappr@gmail.com

The Power of Influence Revealed

Chapter 1

Introduction

Treasured from ancient times to the present, the axiom, "with great power comes great responsibility," reveals comparable ideas in quotes from Greek philosopher Socrates, and English historian John Dalberg-Acton, who respectively wrote about, "the rule of worthy of might," and that "power tends to corrupt, and absolute power corrupts absolutely." There is great power encompassed in one's influence, which many fail to grasp fully. However, this power is accompanied by an ethical responsibility to use it with integrity and purpose. Power devoid of purpose is, indeed, precarious, as it will diminish and ultimately fail.

Lately, I've been thinking a lot about influence. Before I began writing this book, I observed the types of influence that drive everyday people to make everyday decisions. I also found myself reminiscing on those individuals whose influences were instrumental to me throughout my life. I recall that not all who influenced me impacted my life positively. With this realization, I questioned whether I have been wielding my influence responsibly.

My son-in-law, Bryant Lloyd, who co-authored this book with me, told me about his struggles with alcohol that began to take root in him when he was 13 years old. During our conversation, he told me about his late grandfather's nights (and sometimes days) of stumbling home inebriated. He deduced that the years of watching his grandfather, whom he loved deeply, coupled with the closeness of their relationship had somehow impacted his decision to start drinking, despite warnings from other family members. He had consumed his first beer by age 13 and drank sporadically over the years until he was off to college and on his own at 17.

His revelation resonated with me for two reasons. First, because I am a grandfather myself of three young children, and secondly, the close nature of the relationship between my son-in-law and his grandfather. Their relationship reminded me of the relationship I had with my uncle in my youth. My uncle was someone whom I also loved and admired deeply. His lifestyle resembled something out of a movie. Seeing the money, cars, women, jewelry, and respect he had on the streets, it enticed me. I wanted his lifestyle for myself. Though, the lifestyle of a drug dealer is not one a young child should aspire to, I did. Eventually, I found myself doing the same things. A decision I neither regret nor rejoice in.

The above stories from the personal lives of the co-author and myself illustrate a persevering lesson that has been made countless times throughout history by scholars, professors, evangelists and thought leaders alike. And that is, actions speak louder than words.

As I write this chapter I think how my four children and three grandchildren have adopted certain behaviors, likes and dislikes, beliefs, etc., that stem from my influence over them. As I recall on one occasion, my youngest daughter, Serenity, was being scolded by her mom for throwing her jacket on the couch as soon as she came into the house from outside. In her own defense, she quickly rebutted, "But daddy leaves his coat on the couch every day, ("Wow! She threw me under the bus.") I spoke silently to myself, because I had no idea that she was doing it because of me. I could feel my wife's eyes stabbing at me. Yet again I could only chuckle silently as I thought, "Well, she's right."

She, and all my children, watched me do this continuously, so, neither her mom nor I could really be upset with her for doing something she shouldn't do even though she knows not to do it. The power of influence, in this situation, basically trumped what she had been previously taught to do with her jacket, because, as I can imagine by her response, she assumed that since I performed this ritual daily, even though it annoys her mother, it must be okay for her to do as well.

One could make the argument that I am an adult and she is a child, however, by using that logic, we as parents miss something vital. We are supposed to be teaching our children how to be responsible adults. What message are we sending by demanding something of our children that we ourselves do not abide by? We can talk, shout, and scream all we want but the truth is our children will do as we do, not as we say. Moreover, my three-year-old grandson, Bryce, full of love and respect towards me, is also shaped by what he observes me carry out often. During church services, as I expressively preach sermons from the pulpit with a steady stride, or do things like collect the tithe and offering, raise my hands to worship or pray, etc., he mimics all that I do, right down to drinking my favorite cup of MontaVida coffee. He, still tender in his youth, is unaware of my influence in his life. Still, it is nonetheless present and powerful, as is evidenced by his mirroring my actions. Consider for a moment the behaviors (good or bad) that you may be engaged in that someone who looks up to you is aware of, either by watching you or listening to you. They might begin to copy your behaviors and attitudes, not having any idea whether it's wrong or right. They just assume it's acceptable just because they know you're doing it. The power of influence is working constantly in our lives whether we know it or not. And the things we DO every day have a more powerful impact than the things we SAY every day. This is where your responsibility over your power of influence becomes clear. You are going to have an effect. It's up to you to decide which one.

Often influence extends beyond the borders of the family. Four years ago, I joined an up and coming marketing company that seemed promising. I presented the opportunity to a close friend and colleague of mine. As I spoke, I fumbled over my words as I could barely explain the opportunity adequately because I had only recently learned the information. Even still, solely on my word, she joined and became my first partner in this new company and has remained with me to this day. When I asked her what made her join with me all those years ago she told me that she had always known me to be a conscientious person and a man of integrity, so she was willing to take a chance. Her assessment of my character influenced her to willingly join an organization she knew little about. It was this moment that revealed to me the potential of influence in one's own financial life, and how easily someone of lesser integrity could misuse it.

Admittedly, something other than my desire to see individuals reach their maximum potential has inspired this book. That "something" is a bubbling frustration that brewed inside me for longer than I care to admit. It stems from the gross misuse of influence that I've witnessed over the years in life, ministry, and business including the marketing company I mentioned earlier. For instance, there are public figures (athletes, music artists, movie stars, etc.) who neglect their influence by denying it as their responsibility, and community and spiritual leaders who preach hypocritical messages of morality while stealing from their supporters, as well as politicians and business professionals who use their influence negatively for selfish gain.

In my opinion, leadership is not dictatorship where the leader behaves as if they have absolute power, bossing people around, not being liable to the rules and demands they require of others and abuse the power entrusted to them. Responsible leaders are accountable every single day to follow through on what they verbally say. A boiling rage almost chokes me when I think about the widespread self-serving attitudes of leaders today, and I am compelled and inspired to share the information in this book in an effort to raise awareness about how you are being influenced and how you might be influencing someone else. Be it poorly rendered, one's life can be potentially transformed in the worst way, leaving in its wake the wreckage of broken relationships, goals unachieved, unrealized hopes and dreams, and unfulfilled lives. Or, be it consummately rendered, lives can be full of hope, confidence, and affirmation, being impacted in the most advantageous way, and creating in its wake lasting blockbuster success in many areas, if not all.

My desire is for this book to inspire a new generation of leaders in a time of tremendous social uncertainty, to invoke a sense of duty into the hearts and homes of communities, and finally, to redefine what our innate responsibility is to our fellow man. I aim to present and clarify the different categories of influence, and approaches to each, as well as to enlighten minds and change hearts of all who desire to partake of the knowledge given to produce extraordinary success in every area of life. The goal is to positively drive a culture of influence through authenticity, credibility, trustworthiness and effectiveness. The purpose is to broaden your knowledge base and help unlock your potential to accelerate your life, full throttle, on the road to success. It is my hope that you will make full use of the information presented in this book so that your power of influence might prosper you in all that you say and do, and allow maximum results for you and those connected to you. Buckle up and enjoy the ride!

The Power of Influence Revealed

Chapter 2

Types of Influence

As I've stated before, the power of influence is working constantly in our lives whether we know it or not. Influence is a two-way street, meaning that you are either being influenced or you yourself are doing the influencing. Here we will cover how you influence others and how you are being influenced every day also. We will talk about a few factors that make people more susceptible to influence.

Conscious Influence

Conscious influence is when you purposely allow the actions, behaviors, or words of someone else to dictate your own behavior. There are many reasons why one would purposely allow oneself to be influenced. In my experience, I have found that people are commonly influenced by people they like or admire. However, there are other factors that would cause us to be purposely influenced by others, namely, respect for a person's authority. It is defined as "a desire to have or obtain something that someone else has including material possessions or social status; and fear of consequence." Most of us have allowed ourselves to be influenced by all of these reasons at least

17

once in our lives. The issue with conscious influence comes when the person or people we choose to follow are heading down a disastrous path, or we choose to follow them for the wrong reasons. The consequence for these errors in judgment can have devastating and long lasting effects on our character, mentality, and overall quality of life.

Unconscious Influence

Unconscious influence occurs when we unwittingly begin to assume the behaviors and actions of others, or when external forces affect our behavioral responses. This kind of influence rules the day as we are constantly led to action by subtle nudges that have been designed all around us. Marketing adds, social media, and the color of the shirt of the car salesman all affect how we think, feel and inevitably act.

The human brain has a very hard job keeping us functional, a harder job than most realize. The human brains is a truly complex organism capable of many incredible feats, but, in all its greatness the brain's process of figuring out things opens us up to many unconscious signals that are tapping into society. In short, our brains search for the path of least resistance, or shortcuts, when making decisions. For instance, when being introduced to someone new, rather than going through a full information gathering process, our brains search for indicators of their trustworthiness. The neatness of their clothes, the confidence in their voice, how attractive they are, all play a role in determining if we can trust them or not. These indicators make up what we call our instincts. Our instincts are a combination of our innate human reactions combined with our past personal experiences. They act as shortcuts for our decision making process. Marketing experts have mastered these subtle nudges to influence our purchasing decisions without us realizing it.

The other aspect of unconscious influence deals with how we are influenced unknowingly by the people around us. This *social influence* comes into play when we are put in a new social environment and need to adapt. Think about a time when you started a new job, and you began a task you were not sure if you were doing correctly. What was your initial response when trying to overcome your dilemma? You probably found yourself looking at your co-workers to see what they were doing. That was your brain searching for *social proof* to verify your actions as wrong or right.

Social proof is a powerful social influence because it can override what we were taught initially if there is enough proof (other people doing it). This is why peer pressure works so effectively, especially among the young. This is also why development of a good culture is essential to the success of any team.

The effects of unconscious influence on an individual's life can be catastrophic! It can lead to:

The acceptance of ideas based on popularity rather than fact;
Adapting to the habits that we see most frequently whether they are helpful or not; and Denying individuality because of possible backlash from peers.

Unconscious influence can be bad, and the sad fact is there is very little we can do to combat it. It is ingrained in our DNA to be affected by our surroundings and it's a survival method given to us to help us adapt to dangerous and ever-changing environments. So no, we cannot change if we are being influenced or not, but, we can determine what has the most influence on us and our lives, which we will discuss more in detail later.

So far we have discussed how others can influence us consciously and un-consciously. Now we will discuss how we are influencing others on a daily basis. Let us begin by talking about how we intentionally use our influence to move others.

Intentional Influence

Intentional influence is when we purposely utilize methods and tactics to move others to action. Leveraging authority, status, position, or relationships to persuade others typically does this. Some common examples are a wife asking her husband to purchase an item she desires, a police officer demanding access to a vehicle in which he has obtained a warrant to search, and an employee putting in a good word to his manager for a friend. These are examples of relationship, authority, and position, respectively, being leveraged to persuade others to action.

Intentional influence can be a powerful ally if utilized with the right tactics and the right purpose. When using your influence to move others, it is important to consider your motives because you are sending a *deeper* message than you might realize. Are you telling your follower (those you have influence over) to execute an order because it is something they need to do in an effort to better the team and themselves, or because you don't feel like doing it yourself? If we are utilizing our influence while motivated by laziness, fear, guilt, or any other number of negative emotions, then we are showing our followers that we think it is okay to be this way as a leader (your position, influencer). This can damage your brand, authority, or relationship.

Unintentional influence

Unintentional influence, like unconscious influence, works on a variety of different levels. Even the use of intentional influence motivated by the wrong reasons can cause unintentional long-term effects. Unintentional influence is when you have influenced behaviors or actions that you did not intend. Surprise! You have likely unintentionally influenced tons of behaviors at home, work, and during frequent communication with peers. And like most, they were likely positive and negative influences if you were not mindful of them. However, undesired effects of your influence can be remedied by being mindful of the motivations behind our own actions.

Your actions are your number one tool for influence, and our motives send the signals to our followers about how to receive our actions. People can pick up on others' motives fairly easily, so be sure to align your intentions and motives with the best of reasons. Though you cannot control how everyone will perceive your actions, as everyone is subject to their own interpretations, consistent action taken with good, positive motives will be hard to ignore.

To recap briefly, conscious influence occurs when you allow your actions and behaviors to be purposely dictated by someone else. This can be because of the individual's authority or position in relation to you, your personal relationship with one another or from fear of consequence. Be mindful of who you follow and do not allow yourself to be bullied as this will result in nothing positive for your life. Unconscious influence can be tricky to identify as it often occurs without you knowing. Become more mindful of your own actions to gain a better understanding of your behaviors and their source. Intentional influence can be thought of as the inverse of conscious influence as it is now you who is purposely leveraging either your position, relationship, or fear to get a desired action from someone. And unintentional influence is simply you influencing the behaviors of others unintentionally. This short introductory to the types of influence has hopefully widened your prospective on what influence is and how it has operated in your life. The next two chapters are focused on limiting the negative effects of outside influences in your life and maximizing your power of influence to benefit yourself and those around you.

Chapter 3

Limiting Negative Influences

Negative influences can wreak havoc on you, much the same as a virus that infects the nervous system by latching onto and penetrating a host cell to manipulate its function, and copy virus particles until it bursts and infects other cells around it. This forms more viruses. Consequently making you sick and potentially contaminating others who are around you. A person's entire psyche, which includes their personhood and the human spirit (that is, your intellect, emotions, passions, and creativity), are all penetrated and controlled by negative influences. Viruses are too small to be seen by the naked eye, and are hindered in their inability to reproduce on their own. As it is with minute and trifling negative influences, they are not immediately evident and their impact fails to produce significant or damaging effects until a host invasion of increased or repetitive negative influences spills over into a person's psyche, thereby, hindering success in one's own life.

Indeed, negative influences can be just as infectious and harmful, if not more, as a virus. You may be unsuspecting of the wrong influences leading you down a treacherous path because, in contrast to symptoms of a viral infection, indicators of negative influence are not easily recognized. As stated in the previous chapter, it takes time and action to see the disastrous effects of negative influence in your life. So, by the time the symptoms roll in, it can take months or even years to restore the damage done.

In this day and age, we are overwhelmed by all of the stimuli that surrounds us. It is nearly impossible to avoid being affected by it. So, if you cannot help but be influenced by the things around you, then why not ensure the things around you will influence you in a positive way? In order to accomplish this, you first must be able to identify the things around you that are influencing you in a negative way. It is then that you can begin the process of replacing those negative things with positive things and initiate change in your life.

Identifying Negative Influences

Successfully identifying the negative influences in your life is a simple matter of enhancing your own self-awareness. Self-awareness is defined as conscious knowledge of one's own character, feelings, motives, and desires. By enhancing your self-awareness you are becoming more in tune with YOU. Many fail to critically assess themselves on a regular basis. By ensuring that your feelings, motives, and desires are in the right place before you make a decision, you all but guarantee that your actions will have a positive effect on your life and those around you.

One way to help increase your self-awareness and identify negative influences in your life is by paying close attention to your emotions during your daily routines. In Rhonda Byrne's book, *The Secret*, she points out that your emotions act as indicators to your current state of mind. Understanding that thought is the prerequisite to action, we can conclude that an experience that leaves us with a negative emotion has influenced our thoughts in a negative way.

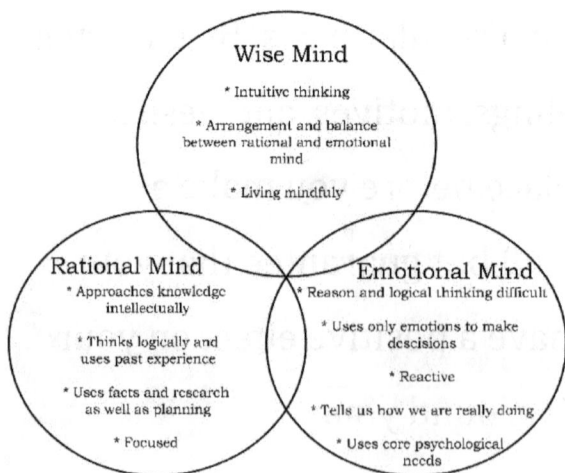

Wise Mind
* Intuitive thinking
* Arrangement and balance between rational and emotional mind
* Living mindfuly

Rational Mind
* Approaches knowledge intellectually
* Thinks logically and uses past experience
* Uses facts and research as well as planning
* Focused

Emotional Mind
* Reason and logical thinking difficult
* Uses only emotions to make descisions
* Reactive
* Tells us how we are really doing
* Uses core psychological needs

As the chart above indicates, listening to our emotions can be a shortcut to identifying some of the negative influences in our lives. Bryant, in an effort to incorporate this philosophy into his life, began to really pay attention to the conversation of those he considered close to him. He noticed a pattern within the context of his friends' and family's speech. One of his closest friends, an individual with whom he had grown up and maintained a relationship into his adult years, had an odd tendency to engage in self-directed putdown humor. He regularly referenced his perceived failures, his lack of money, and his inability to create something of value in his entrepreneurial life in hilarious ways. Having been his friend for years, Bryant realized at some point, that he had begun to mimic this behavior in the same way. After a while, Bryant realized that these "jokes" weren't jokes at all, but, confessions of his insecurities. These insecure thoughts followed him throughout the day, even in his private moments and did not make him feel good about his life. He made an effort to stop making self-deprecating jokes and began focusing on the good in his life and his accomplishments. He also made it a point not to laugh at his friend when he would make these jokes about himself and rebutted it with positive statements about him. Today the same friend no longer makes those jokes, at least not around Bryant.

I have had to practice this philosophy in my business life as well. When I joined the marketing company I mentioned in chapter one, I pitched the company to several people who I considered close to me. It was shocking to me the amount of negative feedback I received in return. One of the most hurtful experiences was when a close relative of mine brought up my past failures as the reason they would not join. I almost let this negative feedback affect me mentally until I really began to notice something. I took a close look at this person and the lives and actions of others who had also given me negative responses, and realized that the source of their negativity wasn't the opportunity, or with me as a person, but within themselves. After this realization, I began to separate myself from those who had self-limiting thoughts, as it would begin to affect me and how I conducted business. The examples from Bryant's life, and mine, show how listening to your emotions can help you identify the negative influences in your life, and how to either limit, or completely eliminate, them from your life. Although your emotions can prove to be a useful tool in identifying negative influences, we cannot solely rely on them. Some of these influences can push you to actions that feel good (or positive) but are in fact bad. These influences can be linked to bad habits and addictions in many people.

The only way to identify the influences that lead you to these actions is to discover what impact these actions have on your life. Author and speaker Jim Rohn once gave a great analogy about doing the wrong things long enough and putting your hand over a flame. Just like putting your hand over a fire and quickly removing it, doing something bad for you just once will have no effect. However, leave your hand there long enough, or continue these bad actions long enough, and the effects will become evident.

Choosing Your Friends Wisely

Speaking of Jim Rohn, he has another philosophy that I have adopted into my own life. He said that, "You are the average of the five people you spend the most time with." I like to put it like this to my listeners during my webinars, "If you hang around five broke people, you're the sixth." Knowing that our environment influences us more than we realize, it should not be too hard to understand how those closest to us affect our behavior more than we credit them. The story about Bryant and his friend's "jokes" perfectly demonstrates how tremendously easy it is for us to adopt the behaviors of those around us. Not only do we assimilate to their habits, but our relationships help shape our thoughts, and affect our self-esteem, as well as our decision-making abilities. Who you choose to spend your time with helps determine how far you go in life. Our relationships either act as propellers, pushing us toward our goals and dreams, or as chains, binding us down to the floor of mediocrity.

While doing research for this book, specifically this chapter, I came across an interesting study that sought the correlation between a professional's industry expertise and the type of feedback they preferred to receive on their performance. The study found that experts in their fields preferred to receive negative feedback while novices preferred positive feedback. The study found that novices required positive feedback to motivate them to continue while experts required negative feedback so that they could continue to grow and change. Taking this information and applying it to how one should decide with whom they spend their time. You would probably come to a different conclusion about who you'd choose if this information had not been applied. Working in my industry, I have experienced so much negativity in dealing with naysayers, doubters, and, for lack of a better word, haters. In my industry we deal with negativity so often that one of the first things we teach new recruits is to change who they spend time around because dedicating time to someone, depending on who it is, can have a significant impact on us either being accomplished in our goals or ridiculously unproductive. Keep in mind that though, in your own viewpoint, you might feel you are extremely clever and highly motivated in your passion to achieve. The doubters, naysayers, and haters will often have a different opinion of you. Since they are not shy in spewing negative words to express their opinions, doubters will only plant—you guessed it—***DOUBT*** in your mind, as I have seen done with many recruits in my industry. Consequently, leading you eventually to give up, which has also proven to be the case with new recruits in my industry. The truth is, when discouragement, suspicion, criticism and a host of other negative influences bombard us like cannon fire, it can be tempting to strike back. It is not prudent, however, to respond to negativity with negativity as it only intensifies bitter feelings and potentially causes you to alienate from others and even from your goals and dreams, ultimately costing you the future prosperity for which you toil. Taking the opportunity to forgo responding to negativity with negativity is indeed wise, but you ought not to stand idly by and allow negative influences and people to tear you down or hinder your progress. Yes! You have every right to refute and guard against every doubter, naysayer and hater. An effective way to do this and keep your dignity intact is to use the very insults and negative actions they hurled onto you as your springboard to catapult into supernova success!

Surrounding yourself with people who support you and believe in your abilities is something that we all require. However, if we construct our circle with only these types of people, we run the risk of surrounding ourselves with *yes men*, that is, those who agree with you despite the truth of the matter. If you only have *yes men* in your corner, you will limit yourself from being challenged and your personal growth will be stunted. Seek to incorporate people into your circle that will challenge you every now and again so you can avoid the toxicity of shiftless thinking, which could hinder your innovative ideas and productivity.

Also include those people who you are certain will tell you the truth about your work ethic, the quality of your latest product or service, and you in general. These people will keep you sharp by pointing out your flaws and helping you to improve them, as well as develop your mental toughness, something you're going to need if you want to reach the top. I do not suggest adding people to your circle who are going to bash you every chance they get (unless that works for you) but someone who is not afraid to share their true opinions.

I myself have found motivation in my naysayers. About a year and a half into my time with the organization, they introduced a health and wellness product line, and encouraged all of us as distributors to adopt a healthy lifestyle so that we would be good ambassadors for the new line. Part of that encouragement was the co-founders' initiating challenge to all of the company's distributors. It was a 55-day fitness challenge, and whoever proved to have the biggest transformation by the end of the challenge would be rewarded with cash prizes. The first-place winner would receive $10,000. At the time, I was far from fit, further than I realized. But, having been an athlete in my youth, I figured I would be able to get back into some semblance of my old form as a running back during my days of playing football. To be considered for the competition, contestants had to submit a before and after photo, complete with all our body measurements and weight. So, while at my home, my oldest daughter and my wife were helping me with completing my body measurements. When I took my shirt off, I will never forget the crackling laughter of my wife and daughter as I stood there bare chested, belly hanging over my belt as they took pictures of me. I knew that they were only teasing and having fun. I never showed it outwardly, but if I am being honest, it hurt me somewhere inside. As they stood laughing and making jokes (especially my daughter), I realized that they had never seen me in my prime. They never knew me when working out was like breathing to me. The athlete in me was aroused by the challenge that their laughter presented. It was then that I knew I would complete this challenge and transform myself, if for no other reason than to prove to them that I could do it. When the 55 days were up, after a rigorous workout routine and diet plan, I submitted my results to the organization. A couple of months after that, during our national convention, I stood on stage and received the *3rd-**place prize*** and a check for ***$5,000***!

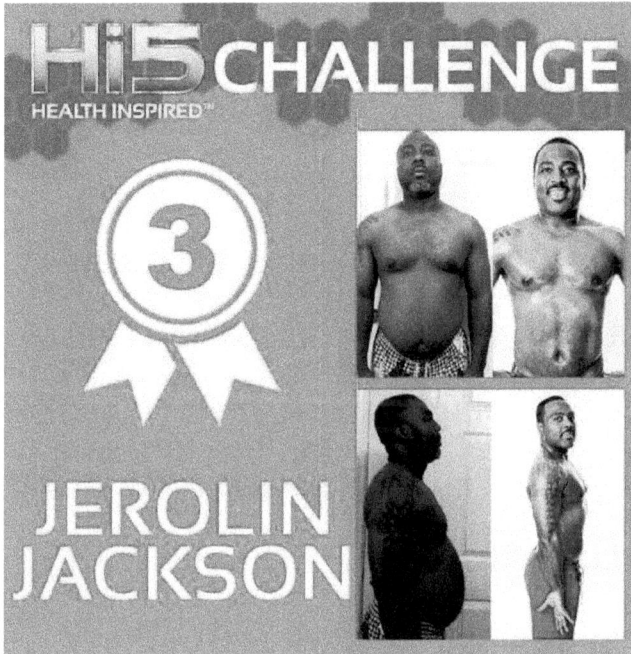

The same competitiveness that drove me as an athlete in my youth drives me as a businessman today. I *LOVE* when people doubt me. Even more than that, I **ABSOLUTELY** love when they voice it. My victory is that much sweeter when I prove the naysayers wrong.

Choosing your friends isn't just about how they motivate you; it's about how they motivate themselves, and what they themselves actually do! If you are constantly around people who do nothing with their day aside from going to work, then you will likely fall in line. There's a saying that goes something like this: if you're the smartest person in your group then you're in the wrong group. Weed the lazy, ineffective, un-motivated, and the gossipers from your circle, they are chains. Relationships that have been forged through years of loyalty can be a hard, even impossible, tie to sever. One thing that you can count on, however, is that once you start focusing on the things that you want in life, your circle will naturally change. Still, you must be alert as to who you allow in. Just because you have the same interests as another person doesn't mean their character is one you want to be influenced by. Become a student of character and you can surround yourself with people who will only propel you into your destiny.

Focus On What's Best For You

Piggy backing off the last section, there is no easier way to limit negative influences other than focusing on taking appropriate action to improve your existence. Conscious and consistent efforts to increase the quality of your life will profit you a windfall of positive changes, as negative influences, by default, begin to naturally fall away and eventually end. When I started working out for the health and wellness challenge, I began by signing up for a membership at a local gym and frequented it without fail. While there, I found people who shared my enthusiasm, who were smarter than I am when it comes to fitness. They gave me tips on how to get the results I needed. I watched to see the things they did every day to stay fit. Even the gym itself, I realized, was a positive environment for me to be in. The walls were covered with healthy alternatives, and positive phrases to get me in the right mindset to exercise. As a bonus, spending more time around these positive places and people took away from the time I spent idly snacking and indulging in activities that led to it.

A few weeks into my workout program, and long before I decided to write this book, I began to notice that something special was happening. My change in focus and consistent action towards my goal began to inspire other people around me. Soon my wife, daughter, and members of my church began to join me at the gym. They began to eat healthy and change their lifestyles. I was beginning to change the very environment I was in on a regular basis by simply focusing on my own goals. The power of influence is an incredible thing when used for your own good!

One way I was able to focus and stay consistent was to give myself a simple task to do every single day. The task I assigned myself was to spend 30 minutes at the gym

EVERY SINGLE DAY, no breaks! Think about the feeling you get on the night of your last day off work. Most people I know are dreading their work day after a nice relaxing break. The next day, you are slow to get out of bed and when you finally do manage to drag yourself into work, it seems to take extra energy to really get into your natural flow again. That same thing happens when you take a day off from pursuing your goals. It just seems to be ***THAT*** much harder to get the ball rolling again. This is because taking that day off has stopped your momentum cold in its tracks. Momentum in your life can only be gained by taking consistent action. Repetition is the key to success. I remember those early days of physical training during the course of my 55-day challenge. My results seemed to come almost daily for the first week. Then the results in my appearance began to wane as time went on. Because I had shed so much body fat early on, the results began to get harder and harder for me to see. Though people who didn't see me on a regular basis could plainly see the evidence of my body changing as a result of my workouts. Nevertheless, I continued to eat healthy, exercise, have weekly weigh-ins, and conduct body measurements, and it proved the ongoing progression of my body, as revealed in the numbers, which helped inspire me to keep going.

When working on your goals you may have periods where it doesn't seem to be going anywhere, and maybe it seems pointless to go on. *Don't stop!* Those are the periods where real growth happens and change begins to manifest in your life. One thing you can do to stay on task is to keep track of your progression. Tracking your progress can give you a sense of accomplishment and provide you with extra motivation to keep going when nothing else will. Staying self-motivated is tremendously important when you're in it for the long haul.

It is extremely important to mentally prepare yourself. Nothing is a momentum killer as not being mentally prepared for what it's actually going to take to reach your goals. Bryant had this experience recently when he released his blog. The initial release was a success and he thought that he had prepared enough to take on other tasks as well as creating new content for his blog and keeping active on social media. A month later, he found out that he had grossly mistaken and had to take an entire month to slowly rebuild the momentum he had at his launch. He considered it a necessary learning experience. He knew zero people who had started and maintained their own blog and built the digital presence that he aspired to, so he could only go by the research he had done... Experience proved to be the best teacher, however, as Bryant learned first-hand what it would take to manage his sites and handle his other obligations, business, and personal life. Now that he knows what to expect he can build and *maintain* momentum.

Focusing on what is good for you will undoubtedly cut a lot of the negative influences from your life. This is partly because honing in on your goals will take so much attention that you will have no time for many of the things you were doing before. The other reason is that your goals should be taking you places where they can be nurtured.

Building momentum is the best way to change your life. The only way to build momentum is by taking action towards your goals every day. When you are focused and have momentum you will begin to influence the people around you to do the same things that you are doing. You will literally begin to change your environment for the better!

In this chapter you learned how to identify negative influences and how to avoid them. You learned the influence that your inner circle has in your life and how to choose who to surround yourself with. Lastly, you saw how focusing on your goals, dreams, and your overall good will eliminate multiple negative influences and replace them with positive ones without you having to consciously do it. Since you have now been armed with the information to limit the negative influences, let's take it a step forward and learn how to transform yourself into a positive beacon of light for your circle by actively becoming a positive influence.

Chapter 4

Becoming a Positive Influence

Part of my inspiration for writing this book was the potential knowledge I could gain on the topic of influence and how I could help others obtain it also. Before working on this chapter, I remembered having the belief that in order to have more effective influence in the lives of other people, I needed to find out what motivated them to action. I believed it was about focusing on people around me and having more of an appreciation for their individual attributes and shortcomings, so that I would be more equipped to help them. At the time it made sense, but as I began this journey of becoming a student of influence, I came to understand that I was mistaken. Yes, in leadership you must know what triggers will catalyze forward movement in your followers. Parents with multiple children certainly may be able to relate to this fact. One child might respond better to positive reinforcement, while the other might need a bit of tough love to get going. Those in a position of authority at their workplace might have reached the same conclusion. Some of your coworkers might respond and produce better results when faced with a challenge, while others fall apart from the stress. Knowing the triggers is essential in leadership, but not in transforming oneself into a positive influence.

Becoming a positive influence is not trying to convince or nudge people to act on the things that will benefit their life. It's committing yourself to living a lifestyle that is so bright with positivity that it becomes infectious and spreads to everyone who encounters you. It's about reflecting on you, not others. Learning and doing things that will positively affect your life on a consistent basis is a foolproof way to surely influence others to do the same. Yes, I do believe we should all strive to become leaders in various areas, such as in our communities, our homes, our workplace, and in our places of worship. Being a leader is *quite different* from being a positive influence. Leaders need to motivate their followers to action because leadership demands results.

A good leader is recognized by what he or she is able to inspire their teams to accomplish, not by the residual effects of their leadership in an individual's life. This might surprise you, but I honestly believe that one does not have to be a good influence to be a good leader. I implore you to earnestly reflect on, and examine your life. I am sure, after doing so, you will agree. Think about the supervisors, leaders, and bosses you have worked for in the past. Think further back to your teachers, counselors and, for some, your parents. There is probably an example of a good leader, a person with the ability to move others to action and get results, who did not influence you positively.

If you're having trouble thinking of someone I will give you an example of a person from history whose passions cultivated a mass following and pushed his country forward by creating a thriving economy and completely ridding it of unemployment. His name was Adolf Hitler.

The way you live your life should inspire others to do more with their own. In this chapter, we will cover the seven essentials to becoming a positive influence: staying encouraged, accepting what we cannot change, having an attitude of gratitude, changing your expectations, building good habits, being action oriented, and keeping your integrity intact. We will break down **EXACTLY** how to use these seven essentials to help you transform into a positive beacon that helps everyone around you be better.

Staying Encouraged

Most of us have lived long enough to know that life can and will throw curveballs at us. There are moments when the stars seem to be aligning in our favor and everything is perfect and then suddenly, ***BOOM!*** Everything around us starts crumbling and we are scurrying to keep it all together. These unpredictable down times in our lives are not only mentally exhausting, but physically exhausting as well. They take an emotional toll on us and can skew our outlook on life. The previous chapter discussed limiting as many of the negative influences as possible that impact your life. However, in that chapter you also learned that it is impossible to eliminate ALL of those influences.

Stress is one of those things that will affect all of us. We can try and eliminate its sources, but it will rear its head at some point or another. The hope that remains is that for those external agitators that bring stress into your life, which you just cannot shake, is to manage them. Learning to manage your stress is the first step to transforming yourself into the positive influence you desire to be. How can you positively influence others if they witness you constantly pulling out your hair from stress? What will happen instead, is either **(a), you will have no impact on their life**

because they view you as someone who is unable to handle your own challenges; or (b), (the most likely effect) you will negatively affect their lives also.

Managing stress is when you arrive at a stressful situation and will yourself to work through it. For example, an employee in a fast-paced work environment might find it stressful to work at the speed required to do the job. To cope with the stress the employee might need to take a 10-minute smoke break to calm his or her nerves. Though this is not a positive coping method, it is all the same a common one. We will cover some simple techniques on positively dealing with stress or stressors that you cannot avoid or change.

Accepting What We Cannot Change

Part of the reason why stressors are stressors is how you think about them. Being in a situation that you cannot change is one thing. Being in a circumstance you can't change that is causing you stress is harmful to your health and psyche. There are some who believe stress is the number one cause of disease and sickness in the human body. I am no doctor, so I cannot confirm or deny that thesis. However, I have seen stress take a physical toll on individuals in my own life, so I wouldn't be surprised if somewhere down the line this theory is confirmed.

Back to the subject at hand, changing the way you perceive a stressful situation or circumstance is an excellent way to help yourself. When my co-author acquired a job at UPS during the holiday season, it put him in an environment with people he was uncomfortable with, and working a job that was physically demanding. This, coupled with the fact that he had to be in the factory anywhere between 2:30am and 4:00am, and having two small children at home, brewed a cocktail for a stressor that could have made him a person that nobody wanted to be around. He was able to combat this by changing the way he viewed his job. Instead of seeing it as something he *had* to do, he began looking at it as something he *wanted* to do. He wanted to do the job because it would provide the capital he needed to get his entrepreneurial ventures off the ground.

Moreover, it would provide him with a way to ensure he would never have to punch a clock anywhere else again. This helped him not only get through his shift, but double shifts and 7-day work weeks as well. The shift in mentality provided motivation for Bryant and helped him to get up and just do it!

Accepting your situation or circumstance is not about just lying down or sucking it up. It's about finding something from it. Find the lesson, the motivation, and the test. Look for ways to turn your situation into a springboard. Take the things that are hurting you and turn them into things that will make you better. With his time being completed at UPS, Bryant can now look back and see that it actually prepared him for entrepreneurship. The long hours, early mornings, and fast pace that the life demands, would have been exhausting for him had he not experienced it with that company. "If I could be at that factory at 2:30 in the morning in December to load boxes, I can get up at three and write." - ***Bryant Lloyd***

An Attitude of Gratitude

Being upset, angry, or frustrated is common. If a person wanted, they could wake up every day mad at the world for a variety of reasons. The economy, the job, the weather, it doesn't matter. What does being bitter accomplish for anybody? To manage stress and become a positive influence you have to look at, well, the positive things in your life that you already have. Health, wealth, family, your looks - anything! Find reasons to be thankful every day. I mean, actually search for them. The world is too full of reasons to be optimistic and grateful for you not to be able to find something. If you can't find something to be grateful for then you're not trying hard enough. Using gratitude as a tool to reduce stress isn't just a theory we cooked up. Studies show that cultivating gratitude can reduce stress hormones in your body by up to 23%. Being grateful literally kills stress!

Change Your Expectations

For many of you, the stressors in your life may be certain individuals that you are unable to avoid being around. Maybe they are a family member you live with or a co-worker on your shift, either way they are around you and are a constant downer. If you have no choice in being around this person or people, one thing you can do is change what you expect from them. If you reflect and seriously think about the issues you have had with other people, I'll bet you can trace the source of the issue back to a failure to meet expectations. Either someone failed to meet yours, or you failed to meet theirs.

We all have expectations. We expect things from ourselves about our future and from people we choose to form relationships with. When people or circumstances fail to meet our expectations we feel let down, taken advantage of, or just plain angry. By altering or lowering our expectations of others we save ourselves a lot of heartache. Take responsibility for your own life and know that you can only control and predict your own actions. Refuse to let others' words sway you, and look for their actions to tell you what you can expect from them. Staying encouraged, essentially, is about focusing on your goals and knowing you have the ability to achieve whatever you set your mind to.

Minimizing stress and negativity in your life helps clear out distractions so that you can keep your attention locked onto what you seek to bring into your life. By accepting what you cannot change, you are enabling yourself to take control of your situation, and even turning it into an advantage. Being grateful improves your mental resilience, helping you to overcome hard times and kill stress. Lowering your expectations of others saves you from being disappointed. Expect the most only from yourself and be responsible for your own life.

Building Good Habits

As stated at the beginning of the chapter, the key to becoming a positive influence on others is by committing yourself to a lifestyle of positivity. Building good habits will lead to good days, which lead to good months and then good years, which ultimately leads to a good lifestyle. The process of building good habits however is not simple. Writing down your goal and then saying to yourself "this is what I am going to do and no one can stop me," is indeed a decent start, but not the answer to changing your life.

One key to creating good habits is understanding that you are not just adding something to your routine, but *replacing* something that is currently in your routine. For example, if your goal is to go to the gym three days a week you must identify what you *will not* do on those days to ensure you make the trip to the gym; such as, watching your favorite show or getting a little less sleep. With that being said, you cannot hope to build good habits without being *specific* about your intentions. That means analyzing not only what you want to do, but also *how* and *why* you want to do it. Last, but certainly not least, in order to truly make it stick, you must surround yourself with a *community* of people with the same goal, or who are invested in seeing you succeed.

Being specific with your goals is the first step to building habits that will actually endure. Making a resolution saying, "I want to be healthier this year" and never expounding on how you're going to get that done is a formula for failure. You might say, "I will eat healthier and go to the gym three times week to accomplish my goal." Though this is a step, it is still not enough. To create a habit that will remain, you must identify *why, what, where, how and when.*

- ❖ **Why do I want this for myself?**
- ❖ **What do I have to do to accomplish this?**
- ❖ **How will I get this done?**
- ❖ **Where will I do this?**
- ❖ **And when will I do these things**

So using the above example of being healthier, a more specific and therefore, more obtainable goal would be; I want to be healthier to lose weight and lower my blood pressure. In order to do this I must *stop* eating fatty and greasy food and drinking sugary sodas. I also must commit to going to the gym at least three times a week and incorporate more vegetables into my diet. I will do this by shopping at organic food stores and becoming a member of a gym within two weeks that is both close and cost effective. I will eat home cooked meals, and go to the gym on Thursdays, Fridays, and Saturdays when my work schedule is lighter. Now that my friends, is a goal that is well on its way to being accomplished!

Replacing parts of your current routine with something more beneficial takes effort and willpower, plain and simple. Have you ever set a goal or resolution for yourself and after a few weeks into it you skip a day, then another, and then *POOF* a month goes by and you have completely abandoned it. One reason for this is because you neglected a key part of goal setting, identifying your sacrifice. Whether you realize it or not, when you set a goal such as working out every day, you are adding onto your already overstuffed day.

Let's use the above example and talk about what you would identify as your sacrifice based on your specific intentions. You can deduce that in order to eat healthy, you must give up the junk and fast foods, but how about the gym? If you go on Thursdays, Fridays and Saturdays, when the work week is light, you may be sacrificing the time you spend relaxing. If you have a high stress, or high activity job, you may NEED that free time to relax and regain your energy for another week of high volume work. At this point you would ask yourself, "Is it worth it?" Will you need that time to gather your thoughts in order to produce high quality work, or can you sacrifice that time to regain your health? If the answer is yes, you can make that sacrifice, then there is one more thing you need to do to make your new goal/habit stick, and that's join a community. As a pastor I see how often people come into church, stay for a little while, and then leave, going back to the same destructive behaviors that led them there in the first place. I've noticed that people who remain and make permanent changes in their lives are the ones who get actively involved with the church. That is because they end up spending more time around people who want them to succeed instead of around the negative influences that led them to the behavior in the first place. Get involved with a community of like-minded people and watch your habit become a fixture in your life.

Being Action-Oriented

People listen to people who do what they say they will do. An action-oriented person is simply someone who will DO first and talk later, if ever. Action-oriented people get the job done. Everyone likes people who can get it done. Not only will people look up to you more, it will benefit you in your career, relationships, and just about every other aspect of your life. Becoming more action-oriented is simpler than people make it. All it requires is doing the things you know you need to do. However, there are some things that can stand in your way. Bryant is a calculating think tank that analyzes everything down to the molecule. Although his way of thinking is useful; it prevented several of his goals from being accomplished in past years. He over-analyzed and missed several windows of opportunity. He had to realize that no matter how much he *thought* about something, it was never going to get done without him, well, actually doing it. He had to accept the fact that he will make mistakes and stumble, but at least, he would be moving. Don't let yourself over-analyze until you're in a state of paralysis. Think, plan, and ACT. Learn to adjust on the way.

Keeping Your Integrity

Getting the job done is one thing. Keeping your integrity, while doing it is another entirely. Can you be honest? Can you stand upright? Can you keep your morals while knocking down your goals? There are some who have compromised themselves so much that the lines between right and wrong have blurred. Morality comes from the soul, and you can only discern between right and wrong by listening to your inner voice.

I did not write this book to preach the gospel, or convert anyone. One thing I do know, however, is that without that guide that's in all of us, none of us would be able to see the direction. Take time to get in touch with yourself. Turn off the news, the radio, get away from the kids and your spouse, and just listen. You can hear more when everything goes silent.

This chapter was full of helpful tips that can help you become that positive influence in someone's life that may not have been available to you. Becoming a positive influence is about focusing on you and developing into the person that people would be proud to mimic. Being a leader does not make you a positive influence and being a positive influence does not make you a leader. Influencing others to live a positive and productive life is one of the responsibilities we inherit with our power of influence. A responsibility that is not as widely embraced as it should be. Those who deny this responsibility deny their responsibility to our future generations. I'm talking about the 99 percent who are inspired through these individuals work but are guided idly with their actions and behaviors in life. There is not enough of these types of people in the world, let you who read this book aspire for something more.

Chapter 5

Tools of Influence

This chapter is unique from the others in several ways. To begin with, we have deviated from the format we used to present and demonstrate the information thus far. Previously, we outlined the contents of the chapter in its introduction before delving into each topic in detail. In this chapter however, we utilize a listicle format. Presenting the information this way will help you focus and analyze each topic individually, rather than as a whole. The grouping method used for the information being introduced is another unique feature of this chapter. In the section entitled *Tools of Influence*, you will see a wide range of tactics, actions, behaviors, and psychological triggers that you can utilize to help influence those around you.

During the course of our research for this book, we came across tons of great literature on the topic of influence from some of the greatest business minds and psychologists in history like, *How to Win Friends and Influence People* by the steel industry pioneer, Dale Carnegie, and *The Art of Seduction* by the wildly popular Robert Greene. We analyzed the methods, tactics, and examples in books like *Influence: Science and Practice,* which delves into the psychology of compliance in the human mind, and tons of other literature such as articles, research papers, social experiments and other mediums. In our studies, we noticed key similarities between these separate pieces. Though some incorporated methods that we considered unethical, manipulative, and not overall matching the core of this book, even those practices would be rooted in these similar ideas, despite being applied deceitfully.

Though the idea for the book is targeted to induce integrity and greater accountability in your power of influence, some of the aforementioned books tremendously pressed upon us the important role of a moral compass and how it plays into influence. These similarities, we noted, could be broken down into simple one word attributes that we dubbed the tools of influence.

A tool is described as a device, or implement used to carry out a particular function. The purpose of the tools provided below is to equip you for the intentional use of each in order to move people to an action that you desire. Before addressing the tools incorporated in this chapter, we would like to provide a word of discretion: that with great power comes great responsibility. Once you begin to familiarize yourself with these tools it may become tempting to use them for less than noble means, transforming these tools of influence into tools of manipulation.

This book was written with the specific intention of revealing to you the power of influence that you already possess. The first four chapters were used to take you through the motions of how influence works in everyday life and to rid you of the negative influences getting in the way of your progression. Now that you understand the power of influence, this chapter and the next will help you wield your influence in a trustworthy manner. As we said, with great power comes great responsibility. Imagine you woke up one day and realized that you have the ability to teleport. With one thought, you could be anywhere in the world - Paris, the beach, the Grand Canyon, inside a bank vault — anywhere. It could be tempting to exploit that power and unethically profit from its use, but with the next thought, teleport somewhere else to avoid any resulting unfavorable consequences. That's exactly the temptation that will come over you once you have been introduced to these tools with the knowledge you have already acquired. This book was written however, in hopes that it will appeal to your sense of purpose. It is for all who desire to partake in and make full use of all that it offers in its intended purpose. We cannot control how you use this information in your own life (if at all). But if you can, just take a minute and reflect on what you want. We could be selfish and use our power to take more and more from the world as several individuals in positions of power have already done, and will continue to do until judgment day. What about actually adding to the world? What about dedicating your life to a purpose, and that purpose being for the benefit of mankind?

How much of a fulfilling life would you be able to lead with that mindset? What kind of life can you create for those who might follow in your footsteps? In turn, what can they do with theirs if they choose to follow your noble path? We, the authors of this book, are not afraid to tell you that we hope to create a legacy for ourselves. A legacy built on the foundation of honesty, love, hope, peace, and prosperity. Will we be perfect? God, no! But we will personally do our best to add as much to the world as possible in the time allotted to us. We also hope to inspire others to do the same. Now, having said that, let's jump into what this chapter is all about - the tools of influence.

Tools of Influence

As stated above, the tools of influence are devices you can implement in your life to move people to action. The list below will outline each tool with a description on how to use them and why they are so effective. The prescribed order of these tools are in no way an indication of the tools effectiveness; rather, it is up to you on how effective each tool can be. For some reading this, many of the tools may come natural in their use. Bryant was taught many of these tools as a child by his mother who spent many years teaching in corporate environments, and his father a real estate entrepreneur who had to form many relationships in order to thrive — more on that later.

1. *Appreciation:* Many of our parents taught us lessons on appreciation. We learned as children that if we said "thank you" and were kind and caring with whatever we had just received, we would likely be able to get the same thing or better the next time we asked for it. By showing people that we truly appreciate them, whether it's their opinion, time, or sacrifices they have made, we motivate them to do more.

Think about your own personal experiences. One instance may be when a special occasion arrives such as an anniversary or Valentine's Day and you decide to go all out for your significant other. You may think tirelessly on what gift to get, what to wear, and take time to prepare a nice meal and set the mood just right for a romantic occasion. Your significant other arrives and they are just too distracted with their phone to notice and appreciate the effort and time you put into the occasion. They eat the food, give you a kiss, and head straight for bed. If this happened to you, what are the odds that you would do something like that again? Slim to none, I'll bet. Whereas, if you were met with love and appreciation you likely would be more willing to do it again, and perhaps not wait until another special occasion.

This is how it works in all types of relationships. If you have employees that you want to motivate to work harder, try investing in an appreciation day once a month for those who do exceptional work.

I'll bet you will notice a higher quality in their effort in the following weeks.

2. ***Names:*** When you see someone you recognize and you really want to get their attention, what is it that you yell out? You shout their name, I'll bet. Have you ever been shouting "Hey!" at someone you recognized on the street who might've been some distance away with their back turned to you? You couldn't remember their name so you just kept yelling "Hey!" until finally their name hit you; then you shouted, "Ashley!" at the same decibel level you had been shouting all along. Then, they instantly turned around? That's because to us our name is the most attention grabbing word on the planet.

You pay more attention when someone says your name during a presentation. Heck, you're more likely to open an email that begins with "Dear YOUR NAME," than others.

When someone uses or remembers our name, we feel special or important, and like we are the center of attention. If there is someone you are trying to influence, make sure to use their name in the conversation. It will make them feel valued, and they will pay more attention to what you are actually saying. People tend to drift during long speeches, so name dropping in a crowd, every now and then, will bring their focus back to you when it begins to wane.

3. ***Interest:*** People show more interest in others who are into the same things they are. People tend to trust others more who have similar interests. In conversation, people tend to be more involved if the conversation is about something that is of interest to them. When Bryant was entering high school he didn't watch sports, his interest was in other things like video games and books. He had a few friends, but he couldn't be part of many conversations because he was less knowledgeable about those things. He even noticed his teachers giving more help to the male students who would trash talk them in class about sports. He told his mom this and she told him that he would miss many opportunities to build relationships if he did not expand his interests. So, he began to watch NFL football and even chose his home team to follow. He played the games, listened to ESPN, and soon was able to hold conversations with just about any guy on the subject of football, which would lead to an identification of other interests. Find out what others like and become educated about it. Doing this will put you in more conversations and help make it easier for you to break the ice, when necessary. Talk about what people love and they will like you more. As we mentioned earlier, people are influenced by people they like.

4. Respect: Respecting other people's time, opinions, position, and points of view will make them feel valued. If you haven't noticed by now, making people feel important and valued are the things that open them up to you. Nobody wants to be disrespected or embarrassed. We all innately want to feel good about ourselves and nothing makes people feel better than being treated well by others. Respect covers a wide range of spectrums. Respecting someone's idea will make them feel that their ideas matter. Respecting their time will make them feel valued.

If you haven't already, you must develop a certain amount of respect for everyone you encounter no matter the circumstance. This is because one, respect is something everyone deserves no matter their circumstance, status, position, or otherwise. Two, you never know who is watching and looking up to you. You never know when that next potential client, asset, or partner will be around and you never know what form they might come in. Show respect and watch it reciprocate in kind.

5. Honesty: People believe in people that they can trust. Being honest, especially when you've made a mistake, will show people that you can, in fact, be trusted and that your interests run deeper than your own personal gain. Don't only be honest when you think it can benefit you. But, be honest when someone asks for your opinion. Nothing is worse than a yes man! Tell people how you really feel without being overly critical, and they will know that you will always be true to them. They may be slightly disheartened when you tell them your honest opinion, but back it up with some words of encouragement so that they feel motivated to improve.

6. Questions: Asking questions is the only reliable way you will ever find anything out about the people you hope to influence. Make your first contact with these people about discovering who they are, what they want, what their goals are, and what their dreams are. Once you know all you can about a person, you can better influence them. Many websites have a questionnaire for viewers to complete in hopes of being able to send them information that can thoroughly help them. There are sites that will actually pay you to answer questions! That's how powerful they are.

7. Nobility: Dale Carnegie said "everyone wants to be glorious in their own eyes." If you stand for something powerful, something righteous, something bigger than yourself (something like we described above), then people will follow you. To be noble is to have high personal qualities and high moral character and ideals. Make your cause something worth fighting for. Give people a reason to support your dreams and ambitions and you will influence them to do so. Religious leaders are able to amass large followings because they appeal to something deeper, something eternal. Your cause however, does not have to be a religious one. The Black Lives Matter movement was able to generate and maintain so much momentum because it spoke to the desire and need of a community that had been ignored for years. Whatever your cause, make it a powerful one. Even something as simple as building a legacy for your family can have the power to move thousands.

8. *Enthusiasm & Emotion:* This hastily moving world is saturated in glitz and glam; so much so, that simple truth will no longer take center stage, no matter how logical it is. You need to add some flare to your ideas to get others interested. Make your gestures exciting while keeping the integrity of your goals. Adding a little emotion into a presentation will register with an audience as long as it is genuine. If you are working for a cause that you truly believe in, then this shouldn't be hard. Find the courage to show others exactly how you feel about what you do and what you want, and you will influence them to join you.

9. *Challenges:* If you want to get the best out of people, you have to present them with a challenge. Challenges are the precursor to success and growth. You want to surround yourself with people who have overcome many obstacles to reach their goals. Find ways to challenge those who you want to influence, but be careful. Everyone is not motivated the same way and if you are overzealous, you can leave people with feelings of resentment towards you. Some can be challenged outright, and some have to be subtly nudged.

10. *Encouragement:* Similar to appreciation, encouragement will motivate others to be and do more. If you constantly fuel people with words of encouragement, they will eventually become courageous!

11. *Boldness*: Fearful people inspire nothing. Bold and courageous action will at the very least put you on center stage where everyone can see and listen to you. Taking a bold stand or creating a product that's unique from everything else in the industry shows you have guts. People like people with the courage to do what they want. The eleven word above are your instruments of influence. They can be utilized in various ways to obtain the same objective, moving people to action. Incorporating them into your work life will help you to not only move up the ladder and reach your goals, it will create a base of supporters that will want to see you become successful and even help on the journey. The tools outlined above are geared to do four things; build relationships, motivate others, deepen your purpose, and stand out. Used properly these tools can accomplish the four above objects and more in every aspect of your life. Find creative ways to incorporate

them in the various areas of your life and
watch your influence manifest and grow.

Chapter 6

Growing Your Influence

Up to now, you have been exposed to a considerable amount of helpful information on understanding your power of influence, and how to utilize it to intentionally influence the people around you. Now, you will learn how to take the power you have and expand it so that you can reach more people. Growing your influence is about extending your area of effect so that you can play an increasingly active role in what and how things influence your life. The larger the capacity of influence in your life, the better you can navigate its course. Be warned however, the larger your area of influence, the more responsibility you have. This is because when you grow in influence, not only is your life affected, but also the lives of those around you. For instance, when a person becomes a parent, he or she bears responsibility for the child, and no matter what, the child is directly affected by the actions and decisions of the parent, even if the parent decides to abandon the child. Consider the leaders of the world for a moment and how many of their routine decisions affect the livelihood of hundreds, thousands, and even millions of people. The president of the United States faces decisions every day that can affect the lives of not only everyone in the country, but of nations abroad as well. "Heavy is the head that wears the crown," a quote which perfectly captures the emotions that can follow one, such as a king, who bears many responsibilities. We incorporated this warning to not deter you from the journey of growing your influence, but instead, to bring home the sense of responsibility that must accompany it. You have likely picked up this book in hopes of changing your life for the better. I encourage you to not only look at it as a way to benefit yourself, but as a chance to be a positive impact on the world at large. Those are the leaders that the world needs, and those are the leaders we hope to help manifest with this book.

Growing your influence is not something that can be done offhandedly. It's true that some people are more naturally inclined to the qualities that make them popular, but to

really grow your influence and to be utilized
for more than just social status, you must be
an active and conscious participant in its
development. Truthfully, this entire book is
filled with information on how to grow your
influence. And becoming a positive
influence, as we discussed in chapter four,
for instance, will attract more people to you,
which you may already be noticing.
People like to feel encouraged and to be
understood so it naturally follows that
people want to be around those who can
make them feel that way. However, this
chapter will focus on elemental keys that
will expand your circle of influence, such as,
identifying your current reach of influence,
developing empathy, providing value,
mastering the art of body language,

becoming a visionary, and getting social. In learning these keys and combining them with what you have already learned, you will begin to see how you can grow your circle of influence.

Identifying Your Area of Influence

By identifying your current area of influence, you are essentially drawing your starting line. Doing this will show you where you are currently, which is a crucial part of any journey (and a journey this is!). How can you reach a destination if you don't know where you are? Getting an exact number of the people we influence is impossible because we just can't know everyone we have an effect on, as your influence on people can be the simple uttering of a single word, or making a certain gesture, or even writing a Facebook post! However, what we can do is take note of the people we are interacting with the most.

Bryant spoke of a conversation he had with a friend of a friend while working on this book. During the conversation, Bryant brought up the theory that we are the average of the five people we hang around the most. This individual scoffed at this theory and rebutted, "What if you just stay in the house all day, what then?" The statement, though somewhat intriguing to ponder, was a moot point. The fact of the matter is we encounter people every single day in various ways, such as through face to face interaction, social media, jobs, school, group activities, family functions, and so on. Our inclination to be creatures of habit means that we will likely visit the same areas and see the same people day-to-day. These very people are likely to be among the ones we influence, or who influence us. In order to differentiate, we must observe how others behave and how we behave around them. Do they seem to mimic your posture and speech? Do they often back up your ideas and agree with you on a number of topics or discussions? If the answer is yes then it is highly likely that you influence their actions and behaviors.

Another way to identify who you are influencing is by taking notice of those who *want* to spend time around you. If you work a typical job you are forced to be around people regularly whether you want to or not. So, if people actually want to be around you then there is a good chance you influence them, even if the signs are not so obvious. Try experimenting with those around you. Do something subtle that is outside the norm and see how people react to it. If you don't already, try bringing a book that you like to work and read it. Take notice of those who ask you questions about it and pay attention to the types of questions they are asking, as they can be good indicators as to how you are perceived in their minds and whether you influence them or not.

Once you begin to get a clear picture of who you influence from those you make contact with regularly, it's time to investigate those whom you influence that may not see you as often. This second tier of contacts should be people you may consider close associates like college buddies who you still connect with from time to time, or someone from a different department, or who works a different shift from you that you have built a rapport with. Contact these individuals and invite them for a night out or lunch, then engage them in conversation. See how well they listen to you. Do they cut you off in midsentence or do they actively listen and ask questions about your thoughts or statements? Are they more into their own thoughts (or cell phone) than interacting with you?

Imitation is a sign of flattery. Take notice if they are mimicking your body language. Do they move when you do? Are they sitting in their chair the same way you are? All of these are clues to your influence reach. Paying attention to the little cues that people give will tell you a lot about what they think of you.

After conducting these social experiments, your circle of influence should now be visible to you. The size of your circle may surprise you, as we likely do not know the people who watch us in silence. If you notice that your circle is considerably larger than what you initially predicted, then reflect on the things you have done up until now to inadvertently win them over. After completing the experiment on himself, Bryant was surprised, not by the size, but by the type of people in his circle of influence. He found that those he looked to for inspiration, which are closely connected to him, had a mutual respect for his ideas and thoughts, and paid closer attention to his words than those he *thought* would be in his circle. This boosted his confidence as the quality of people he influenced was higher than he anticipated.

I myself was surprised after joining the marketing company I have referenced throughout the book by my step-father revealing to me his high regard for my intuition on how to accumulate money. It gave me the added confidence I needed to push forward inside the company and reach my goals. This was primarily because of the high regard and respect I have for him.

Once you have your circle identified, start a list of those whom you feel confident fall into your circle. In my industry we keep a similar list called an active candidate list. We use it to identify potential customers and partners. For you, however, this will be your list of influence. Identify how the people on the list and you can mutually benefit from your relationship and whether or not your influence in their lives has been a positive one. Once you have your circle identified, you can focus on growing that circle even further.

Developing Empathy

Empathy, oh, empathy! Empathy is something that many feel they have, but actually do not, as it is a rarity among people. Empathy is defined as the ability to understand and share the feelings of others. In other words, the ability to truly relate to someone else by understanding what the other person is feeling, and seeing things from their perspective. Empathy could have easily fit into the last chapter as a tool of influence because of the role it plays in creating and nurturing relationships. You cannot have influence if you cannot form strong meaningful relationships.

Empathy is a skill needed to be able to understand the people around you. It's difficult for people to understand those around them because most individuals are too caught up into themselves and their own goals to pay attention to another's. Empathy is about throwing your perspective out of the window so that you can fully put yourself in the other person's shoes. Apathetic behavior toward others, however, exposes us to an underlying flaw in ourselves. We hate being perceived as wrong. Most of us have said it of others and likely we've all had it said regarding us; but, that's because it's true. In an effort to help you combat this, we have put together a few tips on how to develop your empathy.

Be Present

We touched on the topic header above when we detailed how to determine if you have influence over someone or not. When talking to people who are drifting off to nowhere with their nose buried in a phone, or they're just clearly not paying attention, it makes us feel like we are not important or that our ideas are not a factor (at least to them). So when we ourselves respond to others this way, we are sending the same signal to them - that they are not important. When having a conversation, focus on the person. Look into their eyes and listen to their words. Ask questions about what they are talking about, REAL questions not just off-handed comments.

Throw Out Your Views

In this most recent presidential election there was so much bad press circulating about the character of our eventual president, Donald Trump, that many people could not fathom how he gained such immense support. Opinions became so hostile that if someone publicly showed support for Trump they were labeled many undignified names. There were even polls scaling the intelligence of the average Trump supporter floating around. It wasn't until his victory that people realized how many people actually did support him. Despite all the accusations and his failure to win the popular vote, he still had a larger support group going into the last vote than most realized. This happened because during the time before the election, many Trump supporters fell silent about their true views and intentions because of how they would be judged. Imagine if rather than labeling these supporters and making them feel alienated, people tried to truly communicate with and understand these individuals' views. Maybe a conversation could have taken place as to why they actually chose to support Trump to become president of the United States.

When meeting someone or having a conversation, listen to them and open your mind. Do not hinder yourself by your own perceptions. Try to see things as they do. In order to do this, you must take into account the differences between you and them, and know that this is a normal person just like you. They want good things for people and themselves, as most people generally do. They have fears, insecurities and questions just like everyone. Throw away your views for the moment and learn to accept another's. Practicing this keeps you from unfairly judging others as well.

Provide Value

In gaining anything for yourself, provide value to others. If you can offer no value to those around you, you can practically guarantee your influence will have minimal reach. Auspiciously providing value to those around you will enable them to look to you as an asset and therefore be more susceptible to your influence. Notice that individuals with large monetary value attract admirers from around the world, despite the lack of knowledge of the individuals' character. In the film, *The Wolf of Wall Street,* Leonardo DiCaprio depicts

Jordan Belfort as he sits inside a diner enjoying a cup of coffee; when the character portrayed by Jonah Hill, Donnie, approaches him with questions about his work because of the car he drove up to the diner in. After a *very* brief conversation, Donnie tells Jordan that if he shows him a pay stub for $72,000 he would quit his job and work for him. After Jordan slides the stub from his briefcase and shows it to Donnie, the scene jumps to Donnie using a payphone, with Jordan next to him, telling his boss that he quits. The scene is powerful because it displays how the influence of providing value can take effect. Donnie knew little about Jordan and was willing to leave his job to work for him. A decision that eventually lands him in jail, as Jordan was committing fraud to earn those substantial paychecks. If you can provide enough value, it will put you in a position of high regard in many people's minds, despite what they may or may not know about you.

There are many different ways one can provide value. Information has value, money has value, and skill has value. What you must do if you want to provide value is take an assessment of everything you have to offer. Look at your skills, your resources, your contacts, everything! Genuinely take stock in that, and see how you can help people from your current position. Once you begin to get a picture of what you can do for others, you can start to look at your immediate circle of influence and begin to identify needs. Once you identify the needs of those around you, you can start to match what you can offer with what they need. Finding needs and filling them will instantly put you in good graces with many of the people around you as well as grow your influence. When you can help people with their needs they will likely tell others about how you helped them and so on. Try to find a unique skill you possess that can be useful. If you determine that what you can provide does not fill a need, then you must commit yourself to continued education.

Continued education is the process of adding skills and knowledge to your list of value. To stay relevant in this day and age (something you need to do in order to grow value), you must continue to improve yourself. A shortcut method to growing your influence is to grow yourself. The more you have, the more you can give.

Master the Art of Body Language

Body language is defined as the process of communicating nonverbally through conscious and unconscious gestures and movements. A study done at UCLA shows that only seven percent of communication is based on the words we use. The rest is split between tone of voice (38%) and body language (55%).

In order to master what we call the art of body language, you must be able to control the signals that your body sends off, and be able to interpret the signals that others are giving you. Mastering body language is a key element to growing your influence because it can help project the image of yourself that you want without using words. Being able to command attention, have an authoritative presence, and make others feel comfortable around you without saying a word are powerful skills to add to your resume!

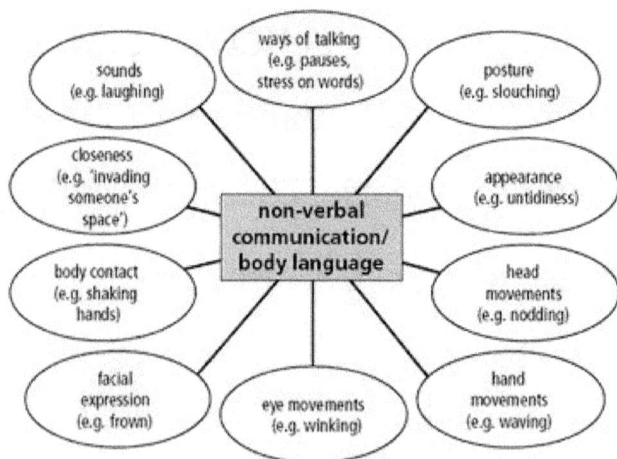

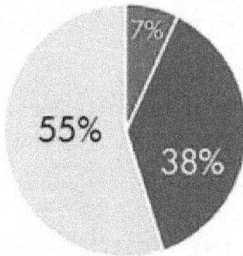

Elements of Personal Communication
- 7% spoken words
- 38% voice, tone
- 55% body language

55%

38%

7%

Source: **Professor Albert Mehrabian**
University of California Los Angeles

Being able to read another's body language plays a huge role in understanding their emotional state during a conversation or how they feel about a situation in general. For instance, when you are communicating with an individual whose arms are crossed, there is a good chance that they are closed off to your ideas or opinions; whereas if their arms are open, the higher the likelihood that your words are getting through. Jittery feet or a jumpy leg indicates anxiety and raised eyebrows show discomfort. In my experience, there are a few signs that are universal among people, but to really understand someone's body language you must begin to understand how that individual thinks. Humans are creatures of habit (I know, I've been saying that a lot) and this fact makes people virtually transparent. Most people do not control their body language in relaxed settings. Observe how your friends and family talk to each other with their bodies and see if you can guess how they are feeling.

Monitoring your own body language is about understanding positions of power, authority, and interest. To exude feelings of authority and power, stand and sit tall, with your shoulders back and head up. The more space you appear to take the more dominant you appear to others. To reach people on a more emotional level you must be able to connect and understand them, which means you need them to open up. Folded arms and crossed legs sends signals of being shut off. Keep your arms open when listening to others, maintain eye contact and nod every so often to show you are listening and interested in what they are saying. Also closing the physical space between you and others will make them feel more comfortable as well as touching a shoulder briefly or shaking hands during initial contact.

Your appearance is not really body language, but it is another nonverbal form of communication. You shouldn't judge a book by its cover, but people do anyway.

Therefore, making sure you appear well put together will make your body language all the more effective. Staying groomed and well-kempt will make you more believable and trustworthy to others. Your clothes are viewed as an expression of self. Make sure your expression is accurate.

Get Social

Did you think you could grow your influence by staying in the house watching TV? You have to get out and meet people who can help you reach your goals. There is no such thing as a pointless trip if it puts you around the right people. For his blog, ThriveIndie.com, Bryant frequents places where there are independent musicians and music professionals. Some trips yield Instagram followers and some yield interviews with high value individuals. He just never knows what reward his social trips will gain him.

Join with people whose goals align with your own. Business professionals should attend every small business owner brunch and social event possible. Grab as many business cards as you can and follow these people on social networks. Follow up with these people by sending them an email or a message on whatever network you follow them on. Attempt to build new relationships with quality individuals. For younger readers, I urge you not to underestimate the power of face to face interactions. No amount of PM's and comments can prepare you for a sit-down meeting with a well-off Chief Executive Officer (CEO) or a powerful potential client or partner. Take as many opportunities to test your knowledge of influence as you can and watch yourself grow.

Become a Visionary

There is a reason we saved this tip for last. Visionaries are the leaders of generations, heroes of stories, and CEO's of multi-billion dollar organizations. They are the ones with "the plan." They are the navigators who are blessed with the ability to see a destination before anyone ever arrives. This coveted title can only be achieved with creative thinking, imagination, ingenuity, and innovation. To become a visionary you must be able to see your goals in life as if you have already achieved them, rather than as something you are chasing.

An easy way to do this is to adopt a solution-oriented mindset. A person with this kind of mindset does not dwell on the events that led them to their current situation or hand out blame to those responsible. They instead look at a problem and only focus on how to solve it. "Push forward!" is the battle cry of all true visionaries, and pushing forward is the action of all true visionaries. A visionary's passion for their dream can motivate others to believe in it too, but marrying that passion with dedication and strategy will move others to be a part of it. The difference between being popular and being a leader is vision. Without a powerful vision and a plan in place to attain it, you have nowhere to guide people to.

Chapter 7

Conclusion

Understanding your power of influence can change your life.

Your influence is a powerful thing. Your influence has the potential to not only shape your life, but the future of the world at large. Think about the effects that others' influence had on your life that you have never met. Leaders and inventors like George Washington and Thomas Edison, writers and poets like Edgar Allen Poe and Langston Hughes. Think of the revolutionary leaders like Harriet Tubman and Martin Luther King Jr., whose influence helped change the very world they were born into. Think about the accomplishments of Barack Obama, and the effects his success will have on our future generations, who do not live in the world where a man of color was never the leader of their nation. What about Alexander the Great and Sun Tzu whose legacy still teaches and inspires the leaders of today despite their lives ending hundreds of years ago? Their potential is your own. They are examples of how far you can climb when you are purpose-driven and dedicated to a vision. They did not accomplish this on their own, however. Their influence brought the people and situations into their lives that were needed to help them climb to their respective positions. Yours can do the same for you.

By paying attention to the conscious and unconscious influences affecting us every day we can begin to move the people and things in and out of your life as needed to help you achieve your goals. Identifying the roadblocks in your way to success is the first step to overcoming them by observing the intentional and unintentional influence you have over others, you can begin to help them be better in their own lives, and inspire them by living to your fullest potential. Once you know what you are doing and how it affects others, you will begin to act more responsibly with your power of influence. Limiting the negative influences in your life will make way for positive change. You must let loose the shackles that bind you to mediocrity. Whether it be those closest to you, the content that you see, hear and read every day, or the words you say to yourself when things take a turn for the worse. Cutting out the old will open up room for the new. You wouldn't put a new couch on top of an old one would you? It's pointless. Create the mental and emotional space you need to add new and beneficial things to your life, and see how things open up for you. Becoming a positive influence is not about trying to change those around you, but about changing yourself. Be the light that you desired in your life. Be the person you always needed when you were growing up. Help others reach their goals and dreams by showing, and not telling, them that it is possible! Staying encouraged and having a positive outlook on things will help you get through the tough times and motivate those around you to do the same. Accepting what you cannot change will eliminate the large portions of stress that derive from worrying. By accepting these things, you can begin to focus more on overcoming and moving away from them, which will boost your own morale and confidence. Changing your expectations will eliminate the excuses you have given yourself all this time. It will make you rely on the only person who can truly change your life, which is YOU. Being action-oriented changes the conversation from what you want to do to what you have done. Stacking accomplishments will challenge those around you to do the same. Understanding and utilizing the eleven tools of influence will guide you on how to positively affect those around you. Appreciating people and the things that they have done will only add to your life. Learning and using the names of the people you want to influence will make them feel valued and bring their attention to you. Showing genuine interest in people will show them that you truly care, while retaining their interest in you, will keep them focused on your ideas. Respecting and being honest with people will earn people's respect and trust for you, you cannot hope to positively influence people if they do not trust you. Asking questions is the only way you will find out what people truly want and need. Having a noble cause will encourage others to follow you, while enthusiasm and emotion will keep them along for the ride.

Introducing challenges to those around you will yield great outcomes, be careful to not be too forceful when presenting them, or risk pushing them away. Encouragement will help others get past hard times, while showing boldness will set you apart and put you on center stage.

Growing your influence is about expanding your circle of effect so that you can better navigate your own life. Once you pinpoint and identify your current area of influence, you can start to see what needs to be done to increase it. Developing empathy will help you to better relate to the new people that will be introduced into your life, as well as the people who are already apart of it. Providing value will make you a commodity. Learn how your unique skills and talents can benefit others. Mastering body language will help you to better communicate. Since 55 percent of conversation is body language, learning the cues and signals that you and others are giving off will help you to decode underlying meanings and emotions. The only way to expand your reach is to get social, and get in front of other people. Put into practice what you have gained from this book by testing it out on complete strangers. Finally, attaining a visionary status will forever change how people view you. Start by practicing seeing yourself in the position you want to be, and not in the position you are in currently.

Parting words from the Author
Jerolin Jackson

This book was created to reveal the power of influence that everyone has, and the innate responsibility we have when wielding it. However, when utilizing and growing your power, we, the creators of this book, hope that you can use it to pursue your lifelong dreams and goals. We want you to develop your influence not just for the benefit of others but for yourself as well. Utilizing your influence to add into your own life is not a selfish act in itself. It's when you corrupt that power by using it in unethical ways for unethical purposes that real harm is done. We believe that part of being a positive influence is living the life that you truly desire for yourself. Living anything less only adds to the myth that we have to settle for less. Go and get your dream and inspire others to do the same. That's our purpose and we hope that this is now one of your goals.

Author & Co-Author Special Thanks:

Leilani Jackson, NC

Robin Taylor, NC

Sha'Tavia Sanders, NC

Serenity Jackson, NC

Lisa Graves, NC

Margo Stuckey, NC **(Mother)**

Kenneth Jackson, NC **(Father)**

Samuel Stuckey, SC **(Step-Father)**

Minnie Scott, NY **(Mother-in-Law)**

Ahondreyea Hudgens, NC

The Rohc Ministries Int'l, NC

The Little Rocher's, NC

Our Lord and Savior Jesus Christ, Heaven

www.ingramcontent.com/pod-product-compliance
Lightning Source LLC
Chambersburg PA
CBHW061725020426
42331CB00006B/1105

9 780998 932415